THE FAÇADE OF FORGIVENESS

AMBER ROWE

ISBN: 9798622590481
ISBN-13: 979-8622590481

TABLE OF CONTENTS

DEDICATION

I dedicate this book to my daughters Amali and Anavi.

I love you. Live in freedom, love and wholeness. No matter the obstacle or challenge you face, I know you will triumph because of your courage, wisdom and boldness. Wax great and always remember that the power that resides in you can never be caged.

"Forgiveness is alive, a synergistic interaction of the mind-body and spirit. All working together to keep you free."

Amber Rowe

My Testimony

Sex Predators

One of my roughest patches was from the age of 14 – 21.

At the age of 14, I lost my virginity to a 20-year-old sex predator who I later found out did the same thing with four of my closest friends.

I never told anyone

At 15, angry and full of low self-esteem, I found myself at the abortion clinic.... this was after I told the father I was pregnant. He ignored me and asked if I would have sex again, but this time with his friend also.

I never told anyone

At 17, I met a guy who was gang affiliated and fell in puppy love, he just happened to be a sex addict. At 19, I broke up with him and decided to begin a commitment to faith. It was a great time until the pastor that baptized me invited me to his home to harvest apples for my family. I asked my mom, she agreed but what she didn't know is that he tried to isolate me in a bedroom.

I knew something was off, and I insisted that he take me home.

I never told anyone

But the new pastor at my church was different. He is young and married, someone I could totally trust. One day he announced a home bible study, and he was looking for hosts. I volunteered and the day of the event nobody came to the study but him and I soon learned he had a fetish for performing oral sex on underage girls and that night I happened to be his target.

I felt horrible and being as that I was newly saved, I asked "will God forgive us"? He replied, "I am a pastor he'll always forgive me I am not sure about you". Heartbroken I went to church the next day and watched him preach and praise God as if we never happened the day before.

I never told anyone

Physical Abuse

Feeling unprotected, I went back to my old boyfriend for support. Before I knew it, he locked us in his room and wouldn't let me leave unless we had sex. I argued with him and shoved my way past him. I made it to the street then BAM! A blow to the back of my head. "Nobody will give a damn about you and nobody will ever love you!"

Disoriented, I looked at him and said, "you will never put your hands on me again, I'm out"!

This was the first time I spoke up for myself and I went home and told my sisters all that had been happening to me. I think that day I cried until I had no more tears to cry.

I finally told someone

When I first moved to Austin, I took self-defense classes and found a love for boxing. I was determined never to be caught defenseless ever again. My trainer would say "girl you hit hard"! But I noticed it draining me so was I out of shape?

Less Brown once said "it's a well-known fact a negative strike has 16x more power than a positive strike". To add to this illustration have you heard of Tai Chi? Well, after a powerful strike, the artist will slowly draw positive energy back in. What I learned from this is that you could be doing yourself more harm than good because I had way too much negative energy going out and no positive energy coming in.

You see, I was fighting to protect myself from the negativity of others more than I was fighting the negativity that resided in me.

I was bitter, angry, unforgiving calloused from pain. I hid behind false forgiveness to shield myself from the wounds of my past.

But over time, I learned that even though unspeakable things happen to me that I still have choices. We can choose to stand up for ourselves and how we want to live out our lives.

I found my greatest healing in forgiving myself because whether I allowed some things to happen or just bad things happened to me, I remained in control of how I wanted the story to play out. Life sucks at times but you are in control of what you make of it.

I chose to release the people that hurt me because, they do not have permission to keep me a victim.

I am *not* a slave to my shame because I am free to be who I want to be, it's my choice and my right.

By the way, I Stopped waiting for an apology.

You may never get it, I can't waste another five to ten years just waiting for a few words to make me feel better about what happened.

My path hasn't been easy, but I keep fighting because now I have two little girls who are watching me. They don't need me to be perfect they need me to be present in my mind, body, and spirit.

I challenge you to face your pain. When you are ready the next pages of this book will assist you on your forgiveness journey. Your story may be tough or, maybe you have no problem forgiving. Either way, liberation is awaiting your arrival.

SUPPRESSION NOT FORGIVENESS

FAÇADE

"An outward appearance that is maintained to conceal or suppress a less pleasant reality."

False forgiveness is basically a kind of forgiveness which does not last, but after a while, it's ugly tentacles of the hurt and resentment that was felt and harbored begin to raise its head once again, and at the end of the day, what happened all the while was just a suppression of the feelings of hurt, resentment or bitterness that was felt then. Suppression is, therefore about the most common facade in which false forgiveness exhibits itself.

Since true forgiveness is expressed by love and not fear, false forgiveness and bitterness that has been suppressed over time will always find its way out on a day to day basis. In suppression, you would notice that there is always a need to find ways to rationalize the forgiveness you intend to dole out to the one who hurt you. Every time there has to be a thought before forgiveness is done, then you can be certain that it isn't a genuine kind of forgiveness. You may be thinking, what's wrong with this approach? There is no right or wrong answer, but to progress in your forgiveness journey, you will need to face the things that you may not be able to see or feel.

Suppressing is simply a mechanism that allows the pain to be hid and "unfelt" for a while. This could become a train wreck because the feelings that you thought were gone would come back into full display. So, what have you been suppressing? It may take a while to recover the thing that you suppressed and that's ok. I really want you to focus on this because you may discover something you weren't prepared to see.

So, let's get back to this word façade.

If you're angry but acting happy, you're putting up a **facade**. A person putting up a façade basically doesn't want the world to know how they're feeling. This behavior can be very dangerous and explosive. Can we all be more honest and assertive about how we feel? Why do we feel that we have to conceal our true emotions like anger, grief or unforgiveness?

My personal experience with emotional facades has been complicated. When I investigate my past, I can see a young girl who doesn't know how to speak up for what she's feeling. I grew up in a household with strong women but at times the same strong women sat backseat to their emotions, needs and desires at times. Life is very interesting because we always say we know what we would do when life happens but sometimes, we don't.

So, one day a few years ago I decided to create a life marker. A life marker can be any day(s) out of the year in which you give complete attention to your self-care. This includes everything from taking personal responsibility for my mistakes or offenses. I also give myself permission to reinforce or shift goals, try new things and pour into my own creative expressions. I chose my birthday because I can be quite consumed with life's responsibilities and being a wife and mother. During these moments of introspection, you discover things that had been suppressed so long that you're a little nervous to dive deeper into what you are feeling. Let me share with you a deep-rooted suppression of my own.

I absolutely love my parents, but for a long time, I had been suppressing anger towards them. When I was about eight years old, my mother moved us from the east coast to the west coast for a career opportunity. My parents never wed, but they co-parented cordially.

In this process, I felt like I had no say, but my father asked me if I wanted to stay with him and not make the move. I wanted to stay with him, and I wanted my mother to stay as well. I had overheard an adult conversation my father was having and instantly thought why isn't he fighting for me to stay with him? As a result, feeling rejected I told him I wanted to go with my mother. I just hid how I really felt as a child to protect myself from feeling unwanted. I didn't tell my mother that I didn't want to go because everyone was doing what was "best "for me. In many ways I always felt tugged along. Of course, my parents had no clue of any of this and they were shocked that I had felt this way.

My husband is an author, and he wrote a book called I Love Anger. His biopic story speaks from a clinical view of anger management, and one day he asked me to take one of his courses for feedback. After taking the course, I realized that I had been hiding a lot inside of me which I didn't know for a long time in my life. So, I spoke with my parents about this over 25 years later and I was able to release the pressure that I had been holding against them for a long time, I forgave and began to heal.

In some cases, the offenders don't even know they did anything wrong. You must gain the courage to speak up about how you feel. My parents knew I loved them and appreciated them, but I had to face the nasty dirt that I kept sweeping under my carpet. My little pile of dirt tuned into a mound over the years and I couldn't ignore it anymore.

My parents were uncomfortable, but I did not want them to be hurt in the present for something they regret that was done in the past. Nevertheless, I had to share and I learned of how they felt during that time. I gained a new perspective that led me to more wisdom, knowledge and understanding that currently supports me now as a mother.

FALSE FORGIVENESS

Because both types of forgiveness can sometimes be difficult to differentiate since they are internal matters of the heart, it is important that you as an individual have the capacity to know when it is true or false forgiveness. Let's talk a little bit about the different facades of false forgiveness. As the waning of the morning sun, so is the fading of peace that false forgiveness brings. The hurt wanes off with the progression of the day only to rise at its peak the next day. Time, they say heals all wounds but never that resulting from false forgiveness. When forgiveness is fake, it brings calmness when the offender is out of sight and a troubled heart once the victim sights the one who has wronged him.

With each day comes offenses thrown at us from friends, family, and colleagues, and so there is always a demand for us to either expend forgiveness to those who hurt us or to remain hurt and unforgiving.

For those with a bit of spiritual tilt, forgiveness is a command that must be done wholeheartedly without denial. This can be difficult because no matter the gravity of offense thrown at you or depth of pain your just supposed to take it. However, a counterfeit kind of forgiveness practiced by some people known as false forgiveness in which the forgiveness granted is neither genuine nor true; rather it comes out of fear and sheer pride. False forgiveness is known to play an equal role spiritually and physically when compared with true forgiveness, as it leads to a gradual depreciation in a person's physical wellbeing, buildup of resentments, anger, and an unbalanced emotional state due to a clog up of memories unreleased. Let's take a closer look at the facades I encountered on my path to freedom.

FAÇADE #1 THE BANDAGE

I am reminded of the funny interactions I have with my daughter about boo-boos. Most of the time when my daughter hurts herself, she comes to me sorrowful and seeking comfort. In the cases where its more comfort than pain I will offer a quick solution. I will offer a pretend bandage, a magical cover that makes every booboo whether real or make believe better. The lesson I learned from my daughter is that fake forgiveness is only a temporary solution to protect your wound. What happens when you keep a bandage on too long? It festers again right. Well, this is why we must not make false forgiveness a permanent solution. The wounds of unforgiveness that you are covering up cannot heal properly because you have not removed the temporary bandage. Exposing the false forgiveness that resides in you is an essential step towards true forgiveness.

Because the forgiveness that was professed was never done from the heart but just from the lips, and it was merely meant to satisfy those around, one key attribute of false forgiveness is the fact that its longevity is usually just temporary. Like the account with my daughter that you just read; it's a temporary fix! As we walk this out, we find that the slightest provocation or offense triggers hurts and offenses that have only been shelved somewhere in mind. When left forgiven, find their way out once again. In false forgiveness, the hurt and pain that is felt does not leave completely but resurface after a while. How long will you allow that old bandage to cover up your pain?

FAÇADE #2

- **Conditionality:**

Genuine forgiveness usually comes devoid of conditions or terms that must be continuously abided by. But this isn't the case when it comes to false forgiveness. It is always predicated on terms and conditions which when breached, exposes the fact that the process of forgiveness had not even began, let alone finished. In false forgiveness, certain terms and conditions need to be met before forgiveness is meted out.

Since false forgiveness has a foundation of terms and conditions, this kind of forgiveness is best described as an agreement which when breached leads to a termination of the agreement.

FAÇADE #3

- **The Past:**

With false forgiveness, the past is shelved and locked until an action from the offender exhumes it all over once again. It may look as though the past and its memories, hurts and resentments have been long forgotten, but that is only an assumption. Because the forgiveness is not authentic, there is still always a lurking desire to get back at the one who offended you by taking out vengeance of some sort.

FAÇADE #4

- **Ego:**

The main motivating factor behind false forgiveness is always ego, and this is the very fuel that keeps it ongoing for years. Unlike true forgiveness that is done because of deep and genuine love, false forgiveness is carried out because of an egoistic idealism, meaning that both kinds of forgiveness are entirely different from each other, and they have their origin in two opposite and different sources. True forgiveness is known to bring a sense of overwhelming peace and tranquility to the soul; but in the case of false forgiveness, that uniqueness of peace and its tangibility is absent in the entire forgiveness process.

- False forgiveness feels like granting a favor to the one who hurt you; you would not mind being applauded for it.
- Another sign of false forgiveness is that it is done out of the fear of losing out on some things.

However, to certify that something is false or true, the original must be well known and identified. So, what is forgiveness?

Forgiveness is a chosen process through which a hurt person decides to let go of his feelings concerning an offense. The victim keeps no record of the wrong acts committed towards them, no matter how hurtful it could be. He seeks no revenge and goes as far as wishing the offender well. Anything outside this definition is not forgiveness. Forgiveness is described as a process because it can't be rushed. It is carried out in phases. The duration for the completion of the process depends greatly on individual differences. To some, it could take days, some weeks and for others, it could run into years. Some are strong enough to forgive instantly while others may need more time. There is no need to rush it because true forgiveness comes with the willful readiness of the victim's heart.

FALSE FORGIVENESS

1. Bitterness

I am reminded of the Sycamine tree, also known as a sycamore tree or mulberry tree. The sycamine tree was a tree that bared fruit that was pleasant and sweet to taste. What is so cool about these trees are their root systems. The systems can grow so vast and deep that they are much larger than the tree itself above ground. Sycamine tree roots have been known to break through concrete cisterns just to get to water.

When I think about this tree, I think about how yummy its fruits could look but also how rotten they could taste. The source of water that travels up into its roots plays a big part in how the fruit will taste. Good source, good fruit and bad source, bad fruit. The fruit could look the same, but the flavor differs completely based on what the tree is connected to.

Do you mean to tell me this tree has a façade? It looks so fruitful but really plain ol' nasty inside! I think unforgiveness is like that. We put on a good face but when we see what were connected to in our spirit, it may not agree with what we think, feel or produce. The truth is that right now many of you reading this are still rooted in unforgiveness. When this is the case, most of what we do depends on triggers. Triggers provoke us to act out and express our feelings. Reactions to triggers could look like:

Someone hurt us in the past, and now our current loved one suffers because of it. Our children are not loved fully because we despised the guardians who raised us. Even a smell or environment can take you back to the moment an offense happened and immediately turn you bitter, depressed or even afraid. Unfortunately, the list could go on and on, there are so many unspeakable offenses that have

taken place in our lives that there is not enough room here to write them all down.

I want to challenge you to think about what could be contaminating your fruit. Like the sycamore tree could your roots be connected to unforgiveness?

_____

_____

_____

2. No peace

One of my colleagues used to have night terrors because during her childhood her mother always went throughout the house opening doors and slamming them. Her mother was checking her clothing pockets for money so she could use it for drugs. So, every time she hears a sound at night like an icemaker tuning up or the toilet seat lid shutting, she wakes up frantically. This leads me to mental health. Let's talk about trauma; I know that it may be tough to admit to yourself that you may have been traumatized, but it's crucial in understanding how to move forward on your forgiveness journey.

3. Mental and emotional trauma

Holding grudges against the one that offended you is like giving somebody free access to the control room of your mind. Unforgiveness can stress you out leaving you vulnerable to physical ailments. The most interesting thing is you end up putting your health in a compromising position when you refuse to forgive while your offender lives serenity and health. As we increase in age, there is a need to free ourselves from roots of worries such as unforgiveness fairly often. Like every other thought of resentment, unforgiveness is detrimental to our health that it could lead to health issues such as high blood pressure, risk of heart, attack and Post-traumatic stress disorder (PTSD).

PSTD is a disorder in which you are always alerted to respond to stress, like leaving your 'fight switch' on all the time even when there is nothing to be fled from or fight against. Symptoms include nightmares; you may begin to see yourself picking a fight with your offender in your dreams every time you sleep which in turn could result in insomnia. Other symptoms are outbursts of anger and mental anguish. I can recall a moment where my husband embraced me from behind my shoulders, and I elbowed him very abruptly. Perplexed he asked "is everything was ok"? I told him that it wasn't him it was just a trigger. In my testimony remember I had a physical abuse where I was struck on the back of my head. Sudden movements from behind often startled me in the past. I am so glad that I haven't had those since I decided to begin my forgiveness journey.

4. Is it all in my head?

It could be very challenging going through all the hurdles of unforgiveness while the person you feel has hurt you is totally unaware of the offence. You risk damaging your health in such a situation. On some occasions, the alleged offender is someone close to you that you can't do without seeing in a day. When they smile, you are mad. They appear untroubled, you are troubled. The silence becomes a torment to you. You end up worrying about their daily activities and ignoring your own life. Have you ever heard the phrase "Don't let anyone live rent free in your head"? It is such a true statement because we allow this to happen. Right now, many of you are thinking about that crush or spouse that broke your heart. You are obsessing about it to no end and the offender probably isn't even thinking about you... at all. Sometimes we waste precious time and energy waiting for an apology we may never receive. You don't have time to continue this way, always remember that only you grant permission for people to hurt you.

TRUE FORGIVENESS

In dealing with false forgiveness, here are some tips that promote true forgiveness.

- Check the motivating factor behind the forgiveness you claim to give; because if it is true forgiveness, then it must be out of pure love, and it can never be bought or sold.
- True forgiveness must always be a gift not a result of any loose gesture.
- True forgiveness is a great source of mental and emotional release for both the one who forgives and the one who's been forgiven.
- Some describe forgiveness as a happy feeling, but this doesn't reign true all the time. Sometimes true forgiveness is a decision you choose to make whether you feel like it or not.

BENEFITS OF TRUE FORGIVENESS

- It helps to promote healthy relationships with others
- Emotional and psychological wellbeing is improved

- Reduced anxiety and stress
- Reduced blood pressure
- True forgiveness may support a stronger immune system
- When forgiveness is genuine, depression is reduced
- Forgiving brings greater self-esteem

IT'S A PROCESS

A true statement from a victim who has been hurt is not an indication that the offender has been forgiven. Most often than none, the victims fight so hard to keep the pain at bay. They act like that incident never occurred like I did. Every time the human nature arises due to unforgiveness, they become so bitter that they require extra grace to suppress the pain gushing out of their hearts. You don't just pretend all is well and leave hurtful situations to fade away on their own. It is not handled by sweeping the feelings under your feet and expecting a miracle to happen. Forgiveness has to be intentional and from the heart. To get started on the journey there are things you must do, and they are as follows;

START WITH SELF-FORGIVENESS

You truly can't give what you lack. To forgive others, you must be good at forgiving yourself. In every crisis, there is always a two-side to the story behind it. No party is totally wrong, and none is totally right. It takes two to tango. If you are involved in a quarrel with someone and things turn around badly, you may begin to blame yourself for this and that. You wish you had never done this or that. You begin to think about the hurtful words that were spoken by the other party and anger sets in. If only you could start by forgiving yourself for every wrong you have done and come into the understanding that the other person is also human.

There is nothing too big or too small to forgive people for. There are some individuals who categorize offence as either big or small, but the fact is that when it comes to true forgiveness, every offence is rated equally; with no smaller or greater than another. This would mean that any offence can be easily forgiven if you are willing.

In the bible there is a passage that speaks of forgiveness that is quite mind boggling. Jesus said we are to forgive 70 multiply by 7 times (Matthew 18:22). 70 x 7 is a lot and reflecting on this scripture over the years, I learned that you may never have to forgive someone that many times but rather the forgiveness that resides in you should be endless and enduring. I think Jesus was more concerned about our mental health in the long-term. This proves that forgiveness is something you need to commit to.   Lack of forgiveness is like punishing yourself for what someone else did to you. Recent studies have shown that genuine forgiveness is no longer just a matter that bothers solely on physical and spiritual benefits but genuine forgiveness which, when embraced, serves as a soothing relief for the soul and medicine to the physical body. Regarding forgiveness and bodily health, it has also been discovered that when people who are hurt, wounded and aggrieved are shown to be led on the path of positivity towards the one who offended. The effectiveness of the cardiovascular region of the body improves, depression is relieved, and there is a general increase in wellbeing.

SPELL OUT YOUR HURTS AND FEELINGS IN CLEAR TERMS

As you step out on the path to true forgiveness, it is important that you are true to yourself about your feelings. Evaluate yourself on the cause of the hurt, when it happened, how you got hurt, and who exactly offended you.

Taking stock of each of these things are critical to the forgiveness process.

This is where a lot of people miss it. They would rather remain angry and offended rather than tackling the origin of the hurt.

AVOID THE HOOK

The betrayal and pain that comes from being hurt could sometimes feel so huge that the thought of revenge or payback feels almost justifiable. But it is vital to know that the pain that is doled out when vengeance is done does not in any way cancel the pain that was received when you were hurt.

DON'T HATE!

Hatred sounds like a negative feeling when it is first mentioned, but the fact is that we are expected to hate something. Hatred is one of the first feelings that come to you when hurt, but it is important that in the process of forgiving genuinely, you are guided carefully in whom you direct that feeling of hatred towards.

Directing hatred towards the person who offended you will do more damage to you than the offender. Walking in true forgiveness requires a lot of courage. When this isn't done correctly, hatred is known to multiply over time, and when it is still not channeled in the right direction, could lead to depression and anxiety.

FORGIVE WITHOUT CONDITIONS

If you are going to forgive. You will be tested to keep forgiveness. Just remember that you are free now and if you go back you are allowing people to live rent free in your mind who are probably not even thinking about you. Just know, remaining in forgiveness to someone means that you have to set healthy boundaries. It helps both sides remain cordial and free from overstepping parameters.

Healing

True forgiveness is a process, and this means it is expected to take some time for a full recovery. During this process of full recovery, it is therefore expected that you open your heart to resources that could help hasten and fortify the process. You may need to visit a counselor, hang out with friends or family members that support your journey without judgment. Your mind must be made up before undergoing the healing process. Sometimes, all you need to heal is the readiness of your heart. One of my favorite examples of healing from something that was self-afflicted or a regret you will find in the scripture below.

In 2 *Samuel 12:13-31*, David consoled himself and stopped the hurtful acts he had subjected himself to when in the actual sense he was supposed to start mourning.

"On the seventh day the child died. David's attendants were afraid to tell him that the child was dead, for they thought, "While the child was still living, he wouldn't listen to us when we spoke to him. How can we now tell

him the child is dead? He may do something desperate."

19. *David noticed that his attendants were whispering among themselves, and he realized the child was dead. "Is the child dead?" he asked.*

"Yes," they replied, "he is dead."

20. *Then David got up from the ground. After he had washed, put on lotions and changed his clothes, he went into the house of the LORD and worshiped. Then he went to his own house, and at his request they served him food, and he ate."*

Finally, I would like to share the 3 most important steps that helped strengthen my forgiveness journey.

SELF-AWARENESS

Much of the unforgiveness I carried was hidden in my own shame and guilt. In my story for years, I never told anyone about my hardships. I was ashamed and disappointed more at myself for allowing things to play out the way they did. I was also angry about the things I couldn't control. And I noticed myself at a young age spiraling into depression. I needed a spiral up, I knew deep in my soul I had to decide to take control of myself, emotions and actions. So, you gotta admit to what happened the good, bad, and ugly and have the courage to face them and get help.

DON'T BE SO HARD ON YOURSELF

Cut yourself some slack reader, do you know how much you have endured up until this point? I need you to grant yourself permission to fail and drop the ball at times. If life were perfect all the time, how would you respond to pain or disappointments? In time, I learned to trust the process even though it was extremely hard at times. I would ask "why me" all the time. I honestly never got an answer, I had much more progress in my healing moving forward than dwelling in the past.

SELF-LOVE

In conclusion, forgiveness is not the same as forgetfulness. Most people expect you to just develop amnesia and forget every wrong they have done to you. No! It doesn't work that way. If you wait until you forget totally to forgive, then you must wait for eternity. Forgetting in this context would only mean not using the past to judge yourself or the offender after you have claimed to forgive. Grant yourself permission to release yourself out of the unforgiveness prison because if you look at your hand

and open it. You will find that you had the key to your freedom the whole entire time.

Please use this space to write your own thoughts about the facades of unforgiveness.

What have you been suppressing?

Do you want to begin releasing this pain now?

What tips from this book can you use to aid your forgiveness journey?

_____

_____

_____

_____

_____

_____

_____

_____

_____

_____

_____

_____

_____

_____

_____

_____

_____
_____
_____
_____
_____
_____
_____
_____
_____
_____
_____
_____
_____
_____
_____
_____
_____
_____
_____
_____
_____
_____
_____
_____
_____
_____
_____

_____
_____
_____
_____
_____
_____
_____
_____
_____
_____
_____
_____
_____
_____
_____
_____
_____
_____
_____
_____
_____
_____
_____
_____
_____
_____

ABOUT THE AUTHOR

Amber Rowe is a professional development coach with over 15 years of experience in the beauty industry. She has an impressive career, which includes working onsite with celebrities at concerts, photo-shoots, and private events. Amber is also a published author and has been interviewed on numerous media platforms, including TV and Radio. Mrs. Rowe has been featured in commercials and has been a guest actress as a result of being a semi-finalist in 2011 for the CW Austin Star talent search.

In her mission to level up and preserve the integrity and future of the beauty industry, Amber realized how important professional development training was vs protocols. She landed her first contract with a multi-million-dollar spa chain and continues to assist spas and salons with employee training and development coaching to ensure providers and the public are safe.

Amber's passion for serving others has also expanded into the non-profit realm; with her husband Isaac, they have been featured on FOX News and The

Washington Post.   Amber and her husband founded **The Man in Me** and **The Women in Me**, both dynamic outreach programs which serve families in the Central Texas Region. Additionally, Amber is a motivational speaker who enjoys encouraging beauty professionals, empowering women's groups, and working with youth to address the pressures leading to teen violence. Amber resides in Austin, where she enjoys life with her husband and two little ones.

Made in the USA
Columbia, SC
18 March 2020